HUNTER AND NOAH VS. SASQUATCH

SASQUATCH CHRONICLES
BOOK 2

PATRICK TALMADGE

HANGAR 1 PUBLISHING

1

THE MISSION IS PLANNED

Hunter, Noah, their dad, and grandpa all tried their best to explain. Dad's company executives asked all three to give their account of what had happened one by one, while the others sat outside and waited, so they could ascertain whether their stories matched up. Their 17-day encounter with the Sasquatch had only lasted 10 minutes to the world outside the valley, so their story seemed fantastic and utterly unbelievable. Grandpa's unexplained beard growth, and the boy's incredibly fast hair growth, highlighted by the fact they had gotten a short haircut the day before, really helped to support their story.

They explained how the Sasquatch had separated the boys from Grandpa, forced him to back out the wall, then made the opening disappear. They explained as best they could that the Sasquatch, no matter how big and scary they looked, had done everything in their power to make sure that neither the boys nor Grandpa were harmed in any way.

The boys went on to tell of how they had gathered berries, fish, freshwater, clams, and slept overnight in trees. They included details like how Noah had tried kicking the Sasquatch, but the Sasquatch remained very gentle. Hunter explained how it seemed that the other Sasquatch found the sight of 10-year-old Noah trying to kick the 8-foot-tall Sasquatch comical—he was sure they laughed—and that they can't climb trees or swim.

Grandpa told them how he figured out that the Sasquatch was somehow able to make the instruments in his crawler read as if it were going downhill when, in fact, he was in some sort of continuous loop that kept him in the area where the boys disappeared. Grandpa went on to say that he wasn't sure if he and the boys had spent the same amount of time out there, because they didn't have any electronics to gauge it with and that too much time had passed to keep track of mentally, especially considering how busy they were.

The company executives did not ask very many questions while the three talked, and those they did ask were mostly just to clarify. After the three concluded their story, the company executives asked Grandpa if he felt that he and the boys would be in danger if they went back and how many Sasquatches they thought there were. They asked if they'd seen them eat anything and questioned Grandpa endlessly as to how technologically advanced he felt the Sasquatch were. They asked him if he knew how it was possible to alter the instruments on his walker. When they started asking Grandpa questions about how the Sasquatch were able to alter time, he just shook his head. Perhaps the executives ran out of questions, or perhaps they realized Noah's patience was wearing thin after he asked a couple of times how much longer it was going to take and said this was the most bored he'd ever been in his life, either way, the executives ended the debriefing.

After spending 4 hours debriefing at Dad's company head-quarters, Grandpa, Hunter, Noah, and their dad went into the lunchroom to plan how they were going to let Mom know her boys had been lost in the forest with an 8-foot-tall Sasquatch for 17 days despite her having seen them that morning. The boys and Grandpa were now being asked to go back out. There was a lot of fame and recognition for the company to consider, and these were the things they also needed to consider them-selves... oh, and Mom. She was really going to be the biggest hurdle for them to overcome before going back out.

Grandpa told the boy's father that he was sure the Sasquatch were harmless, but that they seemed to have a secret plan he hadn't figured out yet. He was also curious about why the Sasquatch wanted the boys only. Why had they pushed him away? Hunter and Noah both told their dad they'd never felt in danger, and that the Sasquatch had done everything possible to avoid harming them. Grandpa assured the boy's dad they were physically safe from harm, but he remained cautious and curious about why they wanted the boys in the first place.

"I think we might want to play down the amount of interest the Sasquatch has in the boys when we talk to their mother. If there is any chance of her letting the boys go on the expedition, everyone needs to remember not to say too much about how the Sasquatch wants them," said Dad.

On the way to take Hunter and Noah home to their mother, with traveling orders from corporate leaders, their dad was nervous. How was he going to convince his wife that it was safe to take their boys into the deep forest to capture an 8-foot-tall Sasquatch? How was he going to explain that they had already spent almost three weeks in the woods with the Sasquatch, even though she would say she saw them leave that morning? It would sound crazy. Well, at least Grandpa's beard, and the boys' suddenly longer hair should help to convince her they had been in a time loop for 17 days, but how were they going to convince her to let them go next time, he wondered.

As they left for home, and the dreaded meeting with mom, Grandpa was racking his brain for an explanation as to why the Sasquatch wanted the boys. It made no sense to push him outside the valley and keep the boys like that... oh, and how had they managed to seal up the wall after they pushed him out?

To say their mother was upset would be a colossal under-statement. If it wasn't for Grandpa's beard, she would have never have even begun to believe the stories, that was until she saw the condition of her sons. When she left them in the kitchen that morning, they were clean and neat, with fresh hair-cuts. Between grandpa's beard growth and the long hair on the boys, there was no doubt they had been gone weeks. They all smelled horrible as well! So, Mom told the boys to go clean up. While the boys were upstairs, Grandpa and Dad tried the best they could to explain what'd happened. The trouble started when they told her their plan to go back with the company and see if they could catch a Sasquatch.

Grandpa was sure that, if he weren't there, the boys' mom would have really been confused and mad that the company wanted to risk her little boys. Grandpa pointed out that the boys had already proved they could outsmart the Sasquatch without help. If Grandpa, Dad, and the corporation's people were there to protect them, then the boys would be perfectly safe. Mom still objected. She said that even with one hundred company men along with them, she would not allow her baby boys to go on the exploration and be placed in such a dangerous situation. Grandpa then said he had an idea, and to follow him.

Grandpa took the boys' parents to his shop to show them a special surprise. He presented Mom and Dad with their own custom Carhartt coveralls. Dad's suit was outfitted like the ones the boys and Grandpa had. It was specially built for deep woods work, except his was outfitted with a few extra specialty tools that included a knife and a sword. Mom's suit was different to everyone else's. It was built for gardening and collecting plant specimens while camping. Though her suit had all the same safety features as the others, the tools were for gardening, not protection.

As Grandpa explained all the details about the suit, Mom's eyes grew wider and wider. She enjoyed gardening, loved tools, and felt her new custom Carhartt suit would make her hobbies easier and more fun. Grandpa had hit it out of the park with that suit and made the chance of her letting the boys go on the expedition hit 100%. She decided to go along with them in her new custom suit. Grandpa and Dad were surprised, and felt relieved they could make the corporation bigwigs happy. Grandpa was glad he'd built the crawler big enough for all five of them, and Mom would be an immense help watching the boys. Grandpa smiled, and went over the workings of Mom and Dad's suits with them, while the boys cleaned up.

By the time Hunter and Noah had finished cleaning up, Grandpa and their parents were back in the house making dinner. While Mom and Dad prepared dinner they explained to the boys the details of their plan. Both boys were excited about their mom accompanying them, and Noah was especially looking forward to showing her how to jump from a tree with the safety reel. Noah was about to tell his mother how he had jumped down into the Sasquatch below, when Hunter subtly kicked him and shot him a "shut up buster" look. Mom didn't notice, and the rest of the evening went off without a hitch.

It took a week for the company to gather all the equipment and personnel necessary to complete their mission. Regardless of how much Grandpa tried to argue that their trip was too dangerous without the government's help, the company heads wanted all the money and press for themselves, so plans were made. The company wanted to capture a Sasquatch and gain worldwide publicity. They insisted on packing nets, cables, tranquilizer darts, and bear spray, even though Grandpa said it was all useless. The company's tech officer passed out laser communication devices, in the hopes that the Sasquatch wouldn't be able to block their signals like they had with grandpa and the boys' electronics. They reasoned that since the laser communicators would send a laser up to a satellite, then the satellite would bounce that laser to the person you wanted to reach, there'd be no radio signals to block. The company employees going on the expedition geared up and made plans to be gone for two weeks.

Grandpa's final surprise was that Hunter and Noah were getting new Carhartt coveralls. They had totally trashed their old ones during the 17 days before, leaving them in such dire need of repair that replacement seemed like the easier option. So, Grandpa built a new set for each of them that were stronger, and with a better safety rope setup. After Noah's experience of dropping down to the Sasquatch and dropping his crank in the process, Grandpa added a fixed crank, a longer rope, and a silent electric motor to make climbing back up faster and easier than hand cranking. Noah was especially excited to try the electric motor out on the Sasquatch, much to no one's surprise! That addition meant batteries would be required, and Grandpa devised a unique method to charge them. On the inside of the sleeves, facing towards the body, Grandpa had woven copper wire, and on the other sides he added magnets. Every time the copper wire inside the arms moved back and forth past the magnets, a small electrical current was generated. It was not a lot of current, but considering how active as a kid is, it would be enough to keep the batteries charged.

2

THE MISSION BEGINS

The company's experts decided there would be no way to sneak up on the Sasquatch, so they decided to use large transport drones to move personnel and equipment as close as the Sasquatch technology permitted. The plan was to fly an empty drone as close as the Sasquatch would allow, and then see what happened. If that drone could land safely, then they would fly the loaded ones in. They had 10 drones, not including the empty test one, and each carried nine passengers and a pilot. The drones could be flown autonomously, or by remote control.

Plans were made to drop Grandpa and the family close to Grandpa's walker, down in the dry riverbed. Grandpa felt it was the safest way for the family to travel after he changed the walker's feet so that it could climb, rather than walk on the riverbed. The company dropped Grandpa, the family, and four workers off, then continued to their drop off spots. The four workers were needed to carry the extra feet for grandpa's walker. Once they installed the new feet, the four workers headed back to the lab to monitor communications.

After they were flown in as close as possible, Grandpa led the group quietly to the walker he'd left in the dry creek bed. It took the four workers 15 minutes to install the new climbing feet. Once they were done, they said goodbye, then headed back to the lab. Grandpa and the family said goodbye and climbed into the walker. Unknown to Grandpa and the family, the four men never made it back to the drone. They were taken prisoner by the Sasquatch, who surprised the men, harmlessly subdued them, then carried them away.

After Grandpa did the outside systems safety check, he climbed into the walker, then began the pre-walk safety check. Hunter, Noah, and their parents climbed aboard and strapped themselves into their seats while Grandpa was finishing up. Once he was strapped in and gave the warning announcement, off the walker went. Everyone had to be thoroughly strapped in because the walker was going climbing. The new feet that'd been installed were really more like hands, since they had steel fingers that could grab. This made climbing like a monkey easy, and it also made it necessary for riders inside to be securely strapped in or they would flail around.

While Grandpa and his family began searching for the best route over the wall into the Sasquatch hidden valley, the remaining nine drones flew to their assigned destinations. While Grandpa was searching, they heard a call come in over the laser communication system to inform them all drones were approaching on time. Grandpa found a small cleft in the wall and headed up through the trees and rocks to the top. The climb up the wall was successful, and as the walker reached the top, the laser system announced all drones had landed safely.

Everything seemed to be going as planned, thought Grandpa, as he maneuvered the walker down the other side of the wall and into the hidden valley floor. Finally, he could relax. After Grandpa's walker reached the valley floor, the laser communication system began chirping like a bird. A few words could be made out, but no complete sentences. The voices sounded excited and hurried, which worried him. Grandpa asked everyone to check their electronics. Everyone reported complete loss of power in all personal electronics. All phones, smart glasses, and smart watches were rendered useless, just like the last time Grandpa and the boys were here.

I'm not happy, thought Grandpa, as he pointed the walker up the valley and towards where they were to meet the rest of the party. Having lost all communication with their group and being in a valley with an 8-foot-tall Sasquatch, the only safe options were to climb back out of the valley or continue to meet the other company members. Dad and Grandpa agreed that if they did not find anyone from the company within 30 minutes, they would head back over the wall and into the dry creek bed.

3

THE COMPANY EXPLORATION PARTY GETS KIDNAPPED

The remaining nine company drones landed in the same dry creek bed, two miles from Grandpa's walker. It was the only stretch of the creek bed long enough to hold all nine drones, 100 feet apart. The plan was to offload everyone, get geared up, then have four of the drones secured in the dry creek bed, while five drones would autonomously fly back to the lab. It was determined that flying the five drones back to the lab would make it easier to send extra supplies and help, if needed.

There were a total of 90 people in the group. Half would establish a base camp in the dry riverbed, and the rest would climb the wall into the valley and meet up with Grandpa's walker. All was going well as the nine drones flew to the drop point. When the announcement came in that the first drone had landed safely, the corporation experts began feeling positive. The message from the corporate office was "full speed ahead." All nine drones landed without incident. After the drones landed, the 10 men in each one began preparing for their tasks. While one group was dressing and getting ready to climb the wall into the valley, the other was offloading equipment to set up a base camp. Being so busy, no one noticed the trouble with their electronics until it was too late. Grandpa and the boys had warned them that electronics would not function inside the valley, and suddenly all the electronics that they had brought along began malfunctioning. One of the drone pilots was the first to notice, when he tried to radio one of the other pilots and couldn't get a signal. The pilot checked his personal radio, watch, and smart glasses. None were functioning. The pilot immediately rushed out of the drone to find his team leader and tell them the news. Before they could do that, a lot of noise and confusion erupted around all nine drones in the riverbed.

The pilot stopped in his tracks, staring wide eyed at what was happening around him. His happened to be one of the middle drones in the line, and on both sides of him he could see large hairy Sasquatch emerging from the woods from all directions. Everywhere he looked, he could see two or three Sasquatch surrounding each person that had come in the drones. Before he could utter a sound, three eight-foot tall Sasquatch surrounded him. Without a sound, he fell unconscious.

The same scene was played out around all nine drones, as the Sasquatch surrounded the people. As everyone fell unconscious, the Sasquatch gently caught each one, then carried them into the valley, and into one of their hidden caves. Once all the people were safe inside the valley, the Sasquatch returned, and flew the drones into their valley. Within 15 minutes, the dry creek bed was completely cleared of all drones, equipment, and humans, and showed no indication there had ever been anyone or anything in it.

4

GRANDPA AND DAD LEAVE MOM AND THE KIDS ALONE

After proceeding through the valley for 30 minutes, with no sign of the company people, Grandpa was beginning to worry. He asked Hunter, Noah, and their mom to stay while he and their dad went ahead to locate the company personnel. Grandpa stopped the walker next to the valley wall, because there was a perfect tree there for them to climb if the Sasquatch came. Grandpa assured Mom that she and the boys would be safer there if any Sasquatch came, because they could quickly climb out of reach, whereas if they were in the walker, they might be trapped.

Mom really wasn't worried about Sasquatch. She still thought the Sasquatch story was too weird to be true. How could there really be huge apes out there that no one had ever seen before? She thought this spot was a perfect place for the boys to eat, so she grabbed their lunch as they clambered out of Grandpa's walker. Mom found a smooth spot with a flat boulder to spread their lunch out onto, so the boys could eat like humans and not like wild Sasquatch. The boys watched while Grandpa's walker disappeared around a corner, and each felt a bit uneasy being left alone in the valley like that.

After eating lunch, the boys began feeling more relaxed and began exploring, while Mom cleaned things up. Hunter and Noah were about 50 feet away from Mom, looking at another interesting tree that went over the valley wall, when three Sasquatch came out of nowhere between the boys and their mom. Noah was the first to see them, and he yelled.

When Mom heard Noah yell, she turned, saw the three 8-foot-tall Sasquatch between her and her children, and yelled. No one was sure what she yelled, but it was loud. The Sasquatch understood immediately, and froze in their tracks. Mom was mad. She was shaking her hands at the Sasquatch, while sprinting towards them. As she waved her arms, the gardening spade in her Carhartt coveralls flipped out like a knife, which she brandished like a weapon. It was hysterical to see this little lady charge at the eight-foot-tall Sasquatch after they tried to corner her boys. Apparently, even they know better than to enrage a protective mother!

While sprinting towards the Sasquatch, Mom yelled at the boys to climb the tree that they were investigating. After the boys were safely up the tree, she turned away from the Sasquatch and sprinted to the tree. The Sasquatch had been frozen in their tracks because of her yelling and obvious anger, so when she suddenly took off running, it took a few seconds for them to react. By the time the Sasquatch reacted, Hunter, Noah and Mom were safely up the tree and out of their reach.

To Mom's surprise, the Sasquatch didn't try to follow them. They must have recognized that they had been outsmarted, she thought, while watching the Sasquatch walk away and breathing a sigh of relief.

"Wow, Mom," said Noah. "Now I know where I got my bravery. That was so cool how they were so scared of you!"

"Yeah, Mom. That was cool," said Hunter. "I can't wait until you and Noah attack them using your new electric climbing gear," he added with a laugh.

"Yeah, ah... no," said Mom. "I think I have had enough of being close to those big fur balls, but obviously, they aren't so tough since a mom can scare them!"

"Well Mom, to be honest, most people—men included—are afraid of you when you're mad! I guess Sasquatch are no exception," said Hunter.

Mom smiled at that, then asked Hunter what he thought they should do since he and Noah had been here before.

Hunter looked at Noah, to see if he had any input.

Noah shrugged, then said "how about we go back to our tree and wait? We can leave a note for Dad and Grandpa telling them where we went."

"I agree with Noah," said Hunter. "We can make a note and hang it from the tree where Dad and Grandpa will see it."

"If you think that's a good idea, my boys, then I'm all for it. I have a pen and I'll write the message on the tablecloth we just used, and we can hang it down like you suggested," Mom replied.

After the note was written and hung so Grandpa and Dad would see it, Hunter suggested they walk along the top of the valley wall instead of going over to the other side like they'd done last time.

"I think the top is flat enough that we can easily walk, and I think we're safer from the Sasquatch as well. Also, we'll be able to see Grandpa and Dad in the walker from the top of the wall, if they come along," Hunter said.

"Sounds like a good plan. Let's get walking to that tree you boys keep talking about," Mom responded.

Noah was super excited that they were headed to his favorite tree. It was the one which they had spent so much time in the last time they were there. He was so excited that Hunter and Mom kept having to remind him to slow down so they could keep up!

It was about an hour-long walk to the tree. When they finally reached Noah's special tree, he raced up so he could be the first to the top and greet his mom when she came up. Hunter laughed, and told his mom that Noah was going to try to talk her into moving into the tree!

Mom stopped walking, put her hands on her hips, and said, "no child of mine is going to live in a tree like a monkey!"

Hunter knew better than to say another word, and turned around to head up the tree to the nest.

Mom followed Hunter up to the treetop nest the boys had built. Noah was sitting on a branch near the edge, with a big smile on his face in anticipation of seeing his mother's reaction. Hunter walked over and sat down next to Noah, and both silently watched while their mom inspected their handiwork. Everywhere she looked, she could see various things the boys had built.

There was a lot of Grandpa's creative genius in these boys, and it was obvious they'd put a lot of thought into designing this nest. They had even brought flat stones up to make a fire-proof cooking spot. She remembered the boys said they had used the reflective foil from their energy bars and a foil emergency blanket for cooking so that they didn't need to light a fire. Mom counted five comfortable looking, nest-like beds around the perimeter, and each had a flat area to keep things on. The boys had even built what looked like recliners, which were covered in soft moss.

After Mom finished inspecting the treetop nest, she glanced over at Noah. The look of expectation on his face made her smile, because she knew he had done all this just to make her happy. Mom walked over to Hunter and Noah, wrapped her arms around them, and said, "this is very, very, very nice boys! Thank you, from the bottom of my heart. We can stay here at least until Grandpa and Dad catch up to us."

Noah could not have been happier after hearing his mother's response. He looked at Hunter, smiled, and said, "I'm going to head down and try to catch us some fish for lunch."

"That was smart, Mom," said Hunter. "I'm pretty sure I didn't anticipate that Grandpa and Dad could be here within the hour, but at least it made him happy."

"Noah's a lot like his dad sometimes, he likes to listen to the parts he likes best, then forget the rest", said mom.

"Well, at least he's doing something useful by going fishing, which means I better get the cooking gear out just in case he's lucky enough to catch something for lunch. Oh, and hey Mom,

I could climb down and get us some mushrooms and huckleberries to go with the fish, if you want?"

"Oh, Hunter... I am amazed at what you boys built, and how well you took care of yourselves while you were up here alone for 17 days. You really demonstrated your maturity, and ingenuity while you were up here. And now here you are about to cook a gourmet meal on top of a tree for your mother! Yes, thank you Hunter, I would love to have wild mushrooms and wild huckleberries with my wild fresh caught fish eaten on top of a tree nest built by my wild sons!"

Mom's voice was brimming with pride and, while Hunter went to gather lunch goodies, she set about fully investigating the tree and found the boys had made nests not just on the canopy of the tree, but under it as well. They had made beds under it by laying broken branches across branches, then covering them with moss and ferns to make a soft bed. Next, they'd woven branches into the area above the beds to better shield them from the rain and help keep it warmer. Mom had to admit, the boys had thought of everything! Everything, that is, except a bathroom with a shower and hot water!

5

NO COMPANY EQUIPMENT OR PERSONNEL FOUND

Grandpa and Dad had been traveling in the walker for 30 minutes, when Grandpa stopped, let out a deep sigh, and said, "this isn't good, there should be 50 people here, setting up a second base camp. I think we need to climb the wall and head back down into the dry creek bed to see what's keeping everyone."

"Then let's make it quick, I don't like leaving Mom and the kids alone any longer than we have to," said Dad.

"I feel the same way. I want her to hurry back, but I know the boys will be safe, they did a pretty good job for 17 days alone, and this time they have their mom."

"Kind of makes you feel sorry for the Sasquatch," said Dad, with a smile.

Grandpa couldn't help but smile at that comment as he turned the walker towards the cliff wall and headed up and over to the other side where the dry creek bed was, and hopefully the company people as well.

As Grandpa was nudging the walker down the wall to the creek bed, he glanced out to the flats where there should be nine drones. He saw nothing but rocks. Dread began to fill his mind. While searching the creek bed for the missing drones and company personnel, all the electronics in the walker—including everyone's personal phones, watches, and smart glasses—came on. When they realized the electronics were working, Dad immediately tried calling Mom and the boys, while Grandpa tried calling the company drones on the radio.

Dad tried calling Mom's phone, and both the boy's phones, to no avail. He tried using the tracker app, but it couldn't locate a signal from any of the phones. Dad was growing extremely worried, and was getting ready to tell Grandpa that they needed to head back as fast as they could, when Grandpa got a response over the radio.

The person who answered Grandpa's call turned out to be one of the experts back at company headquarters. After talking back and forth for five minutes, Grandpa realized that something was wrong. Headquarters had lost contact with all the drones right after they landed. Neither the drone nor the workers who had installed the new walker feet had been heard from since leaving the walker.

Grandpa told the company expert they were heading back into the valley to get Mom and the two boys. Grandpa knew he had to hurry, because time seemed to move faster in the valley than it did in the dry creek bed. If that was correct, then five minutes where he was could be a week for Mom and the boys. Grandpa didn't say anything to Dad about the possible time difference as he quickly pointed the walker back up the wall, into the valley. It was best to keep that knowledge to himself. Why make others worry? They would cross that bridge when they got to it, he thought.

As soon as they hit the valley floor, Grandpa angled the walker in the direction of Mom and the boys and cranked it up to maximum speed. The walker was a combination of both electric and hydraulic propulsion, but it was Grandpa's movements that controlled the walker. He was strapped into a harness and walking on all fours, like a dog, which made the walker move. After climbing out of the valley into the dry creek bed, back up the wall into the valley, and walking as fast as he could for 20 minutes, Grandpa was beginning to get tired. Though he was in good shape, he wasn't young anymore, so he slowed the walker down to take a break.

After two minutes of progressing at a slower pace, they came around the corner to the spot where they had left Mom, Hunter, and Noah. As they approached the spot where they had dropped them off, Dad saw the note they had left and pointed it out to Grandpa. Grandpa headed over to it and they both began reading it.

Grandpa had just begun to say he knew where Mom and the boys had headed to when the Sasquatch surrounded them. One second there was nothing at all around the walker, and the next there were over a dozen Sasquatch. They'd appeared out of nowhere. Grandpa had prepared to meet the Sasquatch the best way he knew how. While Grandpa had gone up the wall into the valley, he had been picking branches and storing them on the belly of the walker for just such an occasion. One by one, Grandpa had the walker's legs grab the branches and shake them at the Sasquatch. Grandpa was going to try to push the Sasquatch away with branches, just like they had done with him. They had proven that they were trying not to hurt him, and he was trying to prove the same thing. The problem was Grandpa didn't seem to be having any luck. The Sasquatch didn't move an inch, no matter how hard he tried pushing them with the branches.

The walker was a large machine, with its main body measuring over eight feet wide and 16 feet long. With its batteries, and fully loaded with supplies, it was easily heavier than two SUVs combined. Each corner of the walker had a large, thick leg mounted to it. Though not capable of moving much quicker than a fast walk, its hydraulic legs were very powerful. Each was easily capable of lifting a pickup truck, but when three Sasquatch each grabbed a leg, they stopped the vehicle dead in its tracks. No matter how hard Grandpa tried, he couldn't make the legs move. The Sasquatch were too strong.

Dad had never seen a Sasquatch before, and Grandpa could tell he was becoming very nervous. Grandpa knew that Dad seeing these huge hairy things was making him wonder what had happened to Mom, Hunter, and Noah. The next thing Grandpa knew, the Sasquatch were picking the walker up off the ground. Grandpa knew the walker weighed well over 10,000 pounds, yet the Sasquatch had hoisted it up with ease. Apparently, the Sasquatch were going to try to carry the walker, Grandpa, and Dad away to places unknown.

Grandpa was pretty sure—well, kind of sure—that the

Sasquatch weren't going to hurt them, but he really couldn't see himself being carried away by the Sasquatch without knowing why, so he decided to use his last-ditch gadget to try and escape their clutches. The ejector seats. Grandpa checked his safety harness, then checked Dad's harness to make sure he was also hooked in correctly, then hit the button.

To say the Sasquatch were surprised would be an understatement. The same could be said for Dad, because he had no idea the walker had ejector seats until he was 150 feet in the air, beneath a parachute, next to Grandpa. Dad was about to yell at Grandpa when he realized Grandpa was laughing like a kid as they slowly glided toward the treetops.

"You should have seen their faces as we took off," said Grandpa, laughing hysterically. "To be honest, I never tested this so I wasn't sure how well it would work, but this is the most fun I've had in years," said Grandpa, as he carefully steered them to a tall tree, and they softly landed in the top branches, far away from the Sasquatch.

"What do you mean, you never tested this thing?" said Dad, as he grabbed onto the tree branches and hooked his safety line on.

"I honestly never thought I would need it," said Grandpa, as he hooked his safety line to a branch, as well. "And honestly, that was so fun!"

Grandpa and Dad watched as the Sasquatch walked away like they'd completely forgotten they were up in the tree. As Grandpa watched them walk away, he sat thinking for a minute in silence until an idea suddenly dawned on him.

"Well, I'll be," said Grandpa. "I know what's going on. I

know why the Sasquatch didn't follow the boys when they were in the trees or on the wall, and why they are not trying to follow us now. The time altering effect in their valley doesn't go all the way up into the trees, just like how it doesn't reach into the dry creek bed!"

"I'm trying not to fall out of the tree here," said Dad, "and you're talking about Sasquatch time paradoxes! All I need to know now is how to find Mom, Hunter, and Noah as soon as possible."

"I wanted to prepare you, in the event mom and the boys were caught in the Sasquatch time altering effect. It's possible that, while we were away from the valley, Mom and the boys went through a greater amount of time than the five minutes we spent down near the dry riverbed... which means it could have been days for them."

"Do you mean to tell me Mom and the boys might have actually been up here for days?"

"I can't be sure, but there's a good chance we were far enough away from the valley to have not been as affected as Mom and the boys were," said Grandpa.

"Well, that means we need to go now, and we need to go fast to find Mom and the boys," said Dad.

"First thing we need to do is get out of this tree, then our best bet is to stay on top of the wall until we reach their tree," said Grandpa. "With any luck, we should reach it in less than an hour."

As the two of them used the electric winches in their Carhartt coveralls to easily climb down the tree, Dad suggested that Grandpa be the one to explain to Mom why it had taken them days, not minutes or hours, for them to return.

"I'm sure Mom will understand after I explain it was the Sasquatches' fault, not ours," said Grandpa, "but then again, maybe you'd better get used to sleeping on the sofa!"

As his feet hit the ground, Grandpa quickly unhooked his safety line and headed down the wall, to the kid's special tree, before Dad could say another word.

6

THREE DAYS IN THE SASQUATCH
TIME ALTERING VALLEY

By the time Mom had finished inspecting all the work the kids had done on the tree, Noah appeared again with three good-sized fish in his hands and a big smile across his face. After she'd finished congratulating Noah on his good work, Hunter showed up with a basket full of huckleberries and mushrooms.

"Oh, my dear boys! It looks like we're going to eat like royalty today," said Mom, as she gladly helped them prepare a delicious lunch.

While they were preparing lunch in their nest on top of the tree, Hunter heard a noise off in the distance. He quietly let Noah and his Mom know that the Sasquatch were drawing near and that they should be quiet. Once he figured out which direction they were coming from, Hunter signaled Noah and his mom to quietly move to that side of the nest and peer over the side. Hunter and Noah had done this before, but this time they were in for a big surprise. The Sasquatch were not alone.

Hunter, Noah, and Mom were so surprised at what they saw down below that they almost called out. It was a group of eight adult Sasquatch, a smaller young Sasquatch girl, and they also had a young, human girl of approximately 13-years-old walking with them. Hunter thought it might be a trick to catch them, so signaled for Noah and Mom to stay silent. The girl was talking to a small Sasquatch as she walked. The group gave no indication that they were looking, and kept walking by.

Hunter waited until the Sasquatch were of view before saying it was safe to talk.

"Who is that girl, and where did she come from?" asked Mom.

"Honestly, Mom, that's the first time we've ever seen her," said Hunter.

"I've never seen her before, but I would sure like to see that young Sasquatch again too," Noah added. "Can you imagine how much fun it would be to play with a Sasquatch kid?!"

"Now I know you two spent way too much time up on this mountain alone, if you want to play with dirty hairy apes," said Mom.

"Hey, I didn't say I wanted to play with dirty Sasquatch, I was just curious who that girl was," said Hunter. "That is the first human we've seen with the Sasquatch."

"You're just curious about the girl because you think she's cute, Hunter," said Noah. "Hunter wants to marry the little Sasquatch girl prisoner," sang Noah, as he climbed down the tree before Hunter could respond.

"You know, Mom, it is strange, because Noah and I haven't seen any humans with a Sasquatch until today. When I first saw her, I thought it was a trap, I thought they were trying to catch us by making us call out for the little girl," said Hunter.

"It's also strange that at no time did any of the Sasquatch or the young girl give the appearance that they were even looking for us," said Mom.

"Another thing that's strange about the Sasquatch when we're up in these trees, is that they have never looked up to where we are, in the trees," said Hunter. "The Sasquatch watches us climb up the trees, but as soon as we're high in the trees, it's like we disappear from their sight, or like they suddenly forget about us."

The boys caught more fish and gathered more huckleberries and mushrooms for dinner. After dinner, Mom, Hunter, and Noah sat in silence on top of the wall and looked down into the valley. It was getting late, there had been no sign Grandpa or Dad, and Mom was beginning to worry. After what seemed like an hour, Hunter suggested everyone head back up the tree and get ready for bed, because night set in early up in the mountains. Noah and Mom nodded their heads in agreement, and everyone silently headed back up the tree to get ready for bed. Hunter and Mom knew enough to be worried, but both felt hopeful Grandpa and Dad were smart and resilient enough to stay safe. Noah, on the other hand, was worry free and content to be sleeping in his special tree again.

By morning, Mom was pretty sure she hadn't slept much. She'd been listening for sounds from Grandpa and Dad most of the night, and worrying about her boys. It seemed like the boys knew what they had to do to stay alive in the woods. At least they weren't going to go hungry, she thought. Grandpa was eccentric, but he'd sure thought of everything while building their Carhartt coveralls. When she lay down to go to sleep, she thought for sure she was going to be cold without a blanket. She could not have been more wrong. Grandpa had added space age insulation to these coveralls so that they stayed cool in the daytime, but warm at night.

While Mom was waking up, Hunter and Noah scrambled back down to get more fresh fish, huckleberries, and mushrooms, plus Hunter suggested they gather some of the freshwater clams he'd found over in the creek. If they managed to catch any, he was also planning on adding a few crawdads to their meal.

It was amazing how much the boys had learned and been able to accomplish while hiding from the Sasquatch, thought Mom. The boys had taken all their training from Dad and Grandpa and applied it perfectly while they were stuck up in the mountains. To say she was angry with Grandpa and Dad about the situation would be an understatement, but they had certainly done a fantastic job of preparing these boys for an emergency, and it showed.

After breakfast, Mom and the boys went down to the water canal to quickly clean up. They didn't want to be away from the great vantage point they had up in the tree too long, for fear of missing a sighting of Grandpa and Dad. They had been back in the tree for an hour when the group of Sasquatch came by again. The small Sasquatch girl and the young human girl were with them again, much to the delight of both Noah and Hunter, but for two very different reasons.

Mom and the boys watched quietly as the incredible procession passed below them once more. Like before, the little human girl was doing all the talking. This time she appeared to be talking mostly to the young Sasquatch, who as far as they could tell never made a sound, let alone spoke a single word. As they watched the Sasquatch company disappear around the corner, they all wondered aloud at the same time who that little girl was, and where she had come from.

The rest of the day and evening was uneventful for Mom, Hunter, and Noah. By the time they all climbed into their nests, no other Sasquatch or human had been seen, nor had they seen Grandpa or Dad.

Hunter could tell Mom was beginning to get a little nervous, so he reminded her that Grandpa had successfully stayed away from the Sasquatch before and that it had taken a couple of weeks for him to finally catch up to the boys, so they just needed to be patient. "Plus, this time Grandpa has Dad's help," added Hunter.

"Yeah, I was kind of thinking about how much help Dad was going to be for Grandpa on this trip," Mom said.

Both Mom and Hunter laughed at her comment about Dad helping Grandpa. After a few chuckles, everyone said good-night and went to sleep for the night. Luckily, Mom slept long and deep that night. After two hard days spent walking, climbing, and being afraid of Sasquatch, Mom finally fell into a deep and much needed sleep.

The next morning was a copy of the previous one. The boys

went down and gathered food for breakfast and then came back up and kept a lookout for Grandpa and Dad until lunchtime. Once more, the boys headed below to get food. After that, while they were making lunch, they heard Sasquatch heading their way. Mom and the boys peeked over the edge to watch. This time there were twelve adult Sasquatch, the young female Sasquatch, and the young human girl.

The Sasquatch were directly under the tree when Hunter realized that the fish they were cooking probably could be smelled from a mile away, and from the looks of those Sasquatch they probably had a sense of smell as good as a dog. Hunter was signaling to his mom that he was worried about the Sasquatch being able to smell the food, and his mom signaled back with a shrugging expression along the lines of, "Oh well nothing else we can do." So, Noah, Hunter, and Mom silently gazed down at the Sasquatch below. Then, much to their horror, the group stopped twenty-five feet away from their tree, then sat down to take a break.

The Sasquatch group rested below their tree for about an hour, during which time not one Sasquatch made a single sound. The young human female, for the most part, never stopped talking. The human girl was talking to the adult Sasquatch and the young Sasquatch girl like they could understand her, and as if they had been answering her. All in all, it was quite an odd sight. Mom, Hunter, and Noah breathed a sigh of relief after the Sasquatch left. The big question on Hunter's mind was how the Sasquatch and the little girl couldn't smell the fish they had cooking up on the tree... they were cooking fish and it smelled up half the forest, yet the Sasquatch did not seem to be aware of it.

"I don't really care why the Sasquatch can't smell the fish, but I am dying to eat my fish right now," said Noah, as he went over to the cooking area to dish up his lunch.

"I swear Mom," said Hunter, "I have never seen a human who thought more about food than Noah."

"I don't know," said Mom, "I seem to remember a little guy named Hunter who used to eat 24 hours a day just last year," she chuckled, then walked across the treetop to get her lunch.

"Did either of you hear what the little girl was saying?" asked Mom.

"I honestly didn't hear a thing. I was watching how the Sasquatch listened intently to her, and I was worried they were going to smell our fish, so all my concentration was there," Hunter responded.

"I know," said Noah.

"And what would that be, Noah?" asked Mom and Hunter simultaneously.

"The little girl's name is Tina, and she kept talking about how important it was for everyone to meet as soon as possible," Noah stated, then continued eating.

"How do you know her name is Tina?" asked Hunter, with a bit too much interest, thought Mom.

"I heard her say her name a few times," said Noah. "Also, it sounded like she wanted to talk to and teach Hunter and I whatever it is they want to teach."

"What kinds of things do they want to teach you and Hunter?"

"I don't know," said Noah. "It was something like ecology, and animal husbands... or something like that, plus other stuff I didn't know and forgot."

"Is there any chance you heard animal husbandry?" asked Mom.

"That's what I said! Animal's husbands."

"Don't try, Mom," said Hunter, "I have learned, it's not worth it sometimes."

Mom shook head back and forth, finally realizing how much Noah took after his dad and grandpa.

"I'm not sure why the Sasquatch want you two, why they want to teach, and why they want to teach you such advanced subjects, but there isn't a chance one of those tall piles of fur will touch my boys," Mom said, in a low tone and with a look in her eyes that would have terrified any Sasquatch.

After a late lunch, Mom and the boys climbed down the tree to wash in the water canal. Mom was going to make sure her boys would stay cleaner than they had during their last Sasquatch outing.

After cleaning up, Hunter led the way to the small river where they'd gathered freshwater clams, and crayfish. Along the way, they filled their food gathering bags with mushrooms, and wild blue huckleberries. Mom instructed the boys to gather nuts as well. If she was going to be stuck in that tree without running water, she was going to make sure she had great food.

On the way back to the tree, Hunter told his mom he had an idea, but it meant he was going to have to run down the canal about a mile, to pick up some PVC pipes and rubber tubing that he and Noah saw last time they were there. Hunter promised it was safe, because he could always jump into the water, like he and Noah had before, then climb out downstream and walk back to the tree. It took some persuasion, but finally Mom relented. Hunter took off as soon as his mom and Noah were safe in the tree. He thought about bringing Noah along to help carry things, but then realized it would worry his mom less if he went alone. Also, if something happened to Noah because of him he would never forgive himself.

It took Hunter less than an hour to return with his treasures. Mom and Noah heard the scraping noise before they saw what it was. It was Hunter, dragging 6 pieces of 20-foot-long white plastic pipe that'd been used for water and irrigation, along with a roll of clear tubing. Once he arrived, Hunter announced to his mom that she was not allowed to come down until he had completed his surprise.

"Ok, Hunter, it's your show, you get to run it. In the meantime, I am going to make a gourmet dinner for my boys."

By the time Mom called the boys to come up for dinner, Hunter had completed his project and was ready to try it out. Mom hadn't noticed Hunter running pipe, hoses, and parts up to the nest, so Hunter was able to finish without her suspecting what he was building. After they had eaten, Mom asked the boys to grab the water buckets, climb down, and bring some water up for cleaning up the area, and to remember to bring the dishes down to clean as well.

"Ok, but first can you look at this, Mom?" asked Hunter.

While Mom was moving towards Hunter, Noah was quietly sitting next to the edge of the nest with a huge grin on his face, obviously waiting for something, she thought.

"Tell me this isn't a snake, or you two will be testing your safety climbing lines! And I'm sure you know what I mean, don't you boys?"

When she saw Hunter's big surprise, she had no idea what it was, and silently stared at the pipes and tubes. Hunter told her he would add a large black bucket, made from a black garbage bag, and some branches woven into a basket, so they could warm water, and Mom could have a warm shower.

"Oh, this is running water!" Mom said, with her eyes wide. "Hunter, you are so smart, I can hardly believe you're only 13!"

Thanks, Mom, I knew you would be more comfortable waiting for Dad and Grandpa if you didn't have to climb down to wash up. Oh, and hopefully tomorrow I can get the warm water working."

"With all this water running up here, don't expect me to bathe," said Noah. "I don't want the Sasquatch to smell me because I'm clean," he added, then headed down the tree.

Mom and Hunter looked at one another and shook their heads in bewilderment at what Noah had said.

"Mom, please tell me I wasn't as bad as Noah," pleaded Hunter.

"I won't say a word... but you can show me how to get running water."

After dinner, Hunter and Noah washed the dishes, then Hunter began weaving the basket that would hold the black garbage bag and provide Mom's warm water. By the time Hunter finished the basket, it was bedtime. Once Mom, Noah, and Hunter finished washing up, they climbed into bed for their third night in the nest. After saying goodnight, everyone fell silent. No one wanted to ask when the others thought Grandpa and Dad would show up.

After they ate breakfast, Hunter asked Noah to help him with a secret plan. Hunter told Mom they had a secret and would be busy for a while. They asked her to stay on the next level below and keep busy while they worked. Mom watched the boys go up and down the tree for the next four hours. Hunter and Noah brought load after load of things up from below, and occasionally they would start laughing, which made Mom even more curious. Mom was beginning to get hungry, and the food was up in the nest at the top of the tree. She asked the boys on their next trip when it was safe to come up and, to her surprise, they said they were ready and were just cleaning the last bits of mess up.

Noah led the way, Mom followed, and Hunter pulled up the rear. By the time she reached the top, Noah was already dancing beside their new addition and singing "we built Mom a really nice surprise" over and over.

They'd woven branches together, lined it with a layer of mud and grass, and filled all the gaps with mud and grass, like a log cabin. The inside was lined with plastic, and the floor was a layer of flat rocks. Coming over the top of the wall was a plastic pipe, like Hunter had used for the sink water, and an old plastic pop bottle with holes in the bottom was attached to the end. After looking hard, Mom realized Hunter and Noah had built a shower for her. It even had a shower curtain!

"I am so amazed and happy with what you two have accomplished!"

"It was Hunter's idea, and I helped a lot," Noah said, happily.

"We made the top out of black plastic and woven branches, so that the sun can heat the water, and you can have at least a warm shower. It won't be hot like back at home, but at least it won't take your breath away," Hunter added.

"Hunter, Noah... this is a wonderful surprise! I will definitely enjoy it later today, once the water is a bit warmer," said Mom, as she hugged her smiling boys.

It was lunch time, Mom was hungry, and she was sure her hard working mountain boys were as well, so she told the boys to run down, get cleaned up, and that while they were at it, to gather a few more berries for lunch.

7

THREE NIGHTS VS THREE HOURS

It was 10 am when they dropped Mom and the boys off. Grandpa's best guess, since he was without a working watch, was that they had been away for three hours. There was no way to know how long it had been for Mom and the boys, and Grandpa was a bit nervous. He was not so nervous about the boys and Mom being safe, it was more about how mad Mom was going to be. That really made him worry!

Grandpa looked ahead of them 300 feet or so, and said, "it looks like we found the boys' tree," then he yelled, "we're here everybody!"

Grandpa and Dad called out for Noah, Hunter, and Mom as they approached. Grandpa was worried that maybe it had been longer than he thought, and that the three of them had headed home down the water way without them. No matter, he and Dad kept calling.

Noah heard voices, and when he realized who it was, he

yelled to Hunter and Mom that Dad and Grandpa were coming. The three of them began yelling at Dad and Grandpa, but it appeared that they weren't being heard. The pair were more than halfway up the tree before they heard the yelling.

"Oh, you are here," said Dad, "why didn't you yell sooner, so we knew you were here?"

"We've been yelling since I first saw you, way down on the wall top," said Noah.

"He's right, Dad," said Hunter, "we've been yelling and couldn't figure out why you didn't answer us until you were almost at the treetop."

"The boys are telling the truth. We have been yelling since you were hundreds of feet away, and you didn't seem to hear us until you were 20 feet away," Mom added.

Dad and Grandpa looked at each other in silence, then Grandpa said, "oh my goodness, the time effect must be different depending on your location relative to the valley. The tree seems to be more affected than the wall top, but less than the valley floor. That means the reason you couldn't hear us, or we you, was that we were in different temporal speeds."

"Once we are far enough away from the valley, our phones and electronics work again, so that might mean once the phones start working then you are out of range of the time changing effects... there must be a way to check this out," thought Grandpa, out loud.

"Let me walk down to the river, past the dry riverbed, until my phone starts working, so I can test Grandpa's theory," said Hunter.

"I want to go, too," said Noah, "I want to travel in time," he added with a smile.

"That's really a good idea," said Grandpa. "It will give us a chance to test my theory, and a chance for us adults to talk while the boys are out."

While Hunter and Noah got ready to go, Grandpa told Mom and Dad, "it will only be a few minutes for the boys while they are out of range of the time changing field, but it may be hours or longer if they stay out too long."

"Wait a minute, Grandpa," said Mom. "So, you mean to tell me the boys can go down to the river, less than half a mile away, and for them it will only be a few minutes, but for us it could be hours... or even tomorrow? Because, if that's what you're planning Grandpa, I am not allowing the boys out of my sight with these big piles of fur running around!"

"I promise the boys will be just fine. They spent almost three weeks up here before, and never saw a Sasquatch outside the valley."

"Well, I swear, if anything happens to those boys, both of you will be hanging from this tree as Sasquatch bait!" said Mom, before going to help Hunter and Noah get ready.

Once Hunter and Noah were prepared, Grandpa instructed Hunter in what they were to accomplish. Hunter was to carry his phone in his hand, and once the phone turned on, he was to count to five and then they were to run back to the tree as fast as possible. Grandpa was hoping that it would only be an hour or two of time difference for the boys, because if it was longer then Mom would have his and Dad's hides, for sure.

As the boys climbed down the tree, Mom and Dad issued

their last warnings for the boys to be cautious. Once the boys were gone, Grandpa started mentally keeping track of the time, then he and Dad sat down to talk to Mom about what had happened so far.

Mom explained everything, starting with how they had been there for three nights. When she got to the part about the girl, Grandpa's face lit up. He was super curious as to why the Sasquatch wanted the boys, and why they had a little girl. Grandpa and Dad explained to Mom what they had gone through and that it had been only three hours for them. When they got to the part where all the men had disappeared, Mom became upset, and asked why they'd let the boys go.

Grandpa did his best to reassure her, "the boys are very safe, and have proven themselves to be resourceful, plus I think the Sasquatch would concentrate on us three since we are nearest the valley."

Grandpa needed to know more about the time effect, plus they needed to talk to Mom about how everyone but them was missing, and do so away from the boys so they could better plan without upsetting them. They needed to decide what to do about the missing personnel. Should they stay and search for the men, or head back into town and get an emergency rescue going? That was the main question, and an added problem was that they now needed to know more about the little girl before they left, thought Grandpa.

Grandpa, Mom, and Dad talked for what Grandpa figured was six hours, and it was getting dark when he suggested they get ready for sleep.

"I can't go to sleep knowing my little boys are out there somewhere, all alone," said Mom.

"Are you sure I can't go down and look for them?" asked Dad.

"No, we can't," said Grandpa. "The boys are in a different time frame or speed, so for them these six hours might have only been a few minutes. My best guess is they will be here tomorrow afternoon, so we just need to stay put and wait."

"I trust your judgment, Grandpa, because you have been here before, and I believe my sons have learned enough to be safe for the night. But, like I said before, if anything happens to those boys, you two men will be in big trouble," Mom said firmly, as she climbed into her treetop sleeping nest.

Mom, Dad, and Grandpa waited all morning for the boys to show up the next day. By noon, Mom was worried crazy and wanted to go find the boys, but Grandpa would not allow them to leave until the boys came back, because he didn't want to confuse the different time frames. When the boys finally showed up, Grandpa guessed it was just past the 24-hour period since they'd left the day before. He wasn't sure how the time differences worked and, if it wasn't for his fear of the danger, he would love to study it more. While Mom and Dad were greeting the boys, and Grandpa was trying to figure out the details of Sasquatch time control, the sound of a voice could suddenly be heard approaching.

8

LITTLE WESTERN GIRL

Noah hurried over to the edge of the nest, looked over, and exclaimed it was Hunter's girlfriend again before Grandpa told him to be quiet. The family watched from the safety of the nest at the top of the tree while the little girl, her small Sasquatch friend, and eight large Sasquatches walked by.

"That girl never stops talking," said Noah, "so she's a perfect match for Hunter!"

Before Hunter could cut back with a response, Mom, Dad, and Grandpa shushed them both so they could listen to the little girl as she walked by. From then on, everyone watched in silence and strained their ears to listen to what the little girl was saying as they walked by.

After the Sasquatch and the little girl left, everyone but Grandpa was talking about what they had seen. Grandpa was sitting quietly, staring off into space, when Hunter asked him what was wrong.

"I have to admit, it's beyond strange to see real Sasquatch, but seeing a small human girl walking with them is mind boggling. That said, what stood out most to me was the clothes the girl was wearing, how she talked, and how she moved," said Grandpa.

"What do you mean?" asked mom.

"I swear the clothes that girl was wearing looked like they were from the 1800s. The way she spoke sounded like she came from the cowboy days, and even the way she moved seemed different to how kids move today."

"I thought she just looked like a cute country girl," said Hunter.

"Ha, ha, ha, I told you so! Hunter wants to marry his cute Sasquatch girl," sang Noah.

Hunter didn't say a thing, just silently threw the pinecone he had been saving for the right moment at Noah, hitting him in the back. Hunter turned away before Noah could tell where it came from.

Before Noah could complain, Grandpa spoke.

"I think she's more than just some country girl, Hunter. I think she's from back in the past, like the Old West. It is possible she has been with the Sasquatch so long that she's actually from the 1800s."

"I mean... do you really think that's possible," Dad asked.

"That means Hunter's girlfriend is an old lady," Noah chuckled.

Again, Hunter silently threw a pinecone at his brother, and turned away before it hit him.

"What is going on?! I keep getting hit with pinecones! I

think the squirrels are attacking me," Noah whined as he stood up and looked around.

Hunter couldn't control himself. He fell into a laughing fit at Noah's confusion. As soon as Hunter started laughing, Noah knew he'd thrown the pinecones, and so began throwing some back at him.

"The next kid that throws a pinecone is going to get thrown out of this tree," barked Mom, as she stood up, put her hands on her hips, and stared at the boys sternly.

Noah laughed out loud, ran to the edge of the nest, attached his safety line to a thick branch, threw a pinecone at Hunter, looked at his mom and yelled, "catch me if you can!"

Then he jumped out of the nest. Mom screamed as Noah did that, forgetting he had a safety line with an inertial reel system attached that would slowly lower him to the ground below. When she finally realized what he had done, she got up, hooked her safety line to another thick branch, looked at the others in the nest, and said, "I am so going to get that kid," then jumped.

The three who remained in the nest sat silently and watched Mom jump.

"I am so glad that isn't me she's chasing," said Hunter.

"I'll second that," said Dad, "I have been on the receiving end of her anger before and would prefer not to repeat the experience!"

Grandpa didn't say a word after Noah and Mom jumped. He was lost in thought about the little western girl. "You know, it's possible that little girl has been with the Sasquatch for over 100 years, and they have somehow kept her from aging... if they can locally control time, it should be a no brainer for the Sasquatch to stop her from aging," he said, wistfully.

"Are you telling me that girl could have been born in the 1800's and could be over 100 years old?" asked Dad.

"How is it possible for that girl to be over 100 years old and look so young, Grandpa?" asked Hunter.

"If the Sasquatch can control time and aging, they could easily keep her young, but for what reason is something I can't say. If she doesn't have a family here, then she wouldn't know anyone alive, so why keep her young? Without asking her we'll never know for sure, so I think we should consider going down and talking to the little girl."

"Do you think it's safe to do that, Grandpa?" asked Hunter. "Those Sasquatch still scare me."

"I am also seriously concerned about our safety after our experience back in your crawler, and this time it's not just you and I, plus we won't have an ejector seat to save us," Dad added.

"All I can say," said grandpa, "is that every indication we have from the Sasquatch, is they mean us no harm. Not once have they laid a hand, or should I say a paw, on us. They held the crawler down, yes, but appeared to not want to hurt us. I am thinking they could simply want to communicate with us, and possibly through the western girl. We need to figure out a way to meet the girl."

Before anyone could say another word, Noah came scrambling up into the nest breathing hard, laughing even harder, and then collapsed into his bed nest. Mom was only seconds behind him, just as breathless and laughing so hard she was crying. She didn't make it to her bed, and laid down next to Dad, laughing so hard she couldn't talk.

"Oh my gosh! That was the most fun I have ever had," Mom said, when she could finally take a breath. "As soon as I catch my breath, I am jumping again," and oh, Dad, you need to jump down with me next time. It is an absolute blast!"

Dad was looking down at her with a confused look on his face while she laughed. Hunter and Grandpa shook their heads in disbelief at Mom. No one had ever seen her behaving so childishly.

"I don't know about Dad, but I am with you on the next jump," said Grandpa. "No one is going to call me an old fuddy duddy!"

After Mom and Noah caught their breath, Grandpa suggested they have dinner. It would give them the chance to plan their next moves, and he was getting hungry since he and Dad hadn't eaten lunch. While Mom and Noah were preparing dinner, Hunter showed Grandpa and Dad everything they had built in the tree top nest, including the luxurious new shower Mom was going to enjoy before bed that night. Grandpa was especially impressed by the solar oven and kitchen they had built.

"I am beyond proud of you two boys. Not only did you survive out here alone, but you also built a comfortable home, and I can tell your mother is proud of you as well," Dad said, with a broad smile across his face. After dinner, the males went down to the water canal so that Mom could have privacy for her first shower in 4 days. After that, and after a bit of family talk, everyone climbed into their nests to sleep.

"Grandpa, I have to admit, not only did you make an incredibly fun electric safety rope, but you also made the Carhartt coveralls perfect for sleeping in," said Mom, as she snuggled into her grass and moss filled nest beside Dad.

"I think the best part is my new Carhartt coveralls have a better slingshot, because this one has a built-in reel and special arrows! I can catch fish with it," added Noah, as he settled into his nest.

"I want to take a moment to thank Hunter and Noah for doing such a great job of building such a fine home away from home. It is comfortable, well thought out, and even has running water, which I can barely believe Hunter was able to pull off with such limited resources," said Grandpa.

"Good night," said Dad. "It has been a tough time for everyone, especially Mom and you boys. Let's get some good restful sleep tonight and make our plans tomorrow when we are fresh."

9

FAMILY MEETING IN THE TREE TOP NEST

Morning came, and with its first and the sounds of crows flying overhead and squawking up a racket could be heard. Grandpa assumed the birds saw some of their food that was accidentally left out. No one would make that mistake again, he thought, at least if they wanted to get a full night's sleep.

After breakfast, Noah heard a familiar sound off in the distance and clambered down to the lower level for a better look, then said, "Hunter! Your girlfriend is coming, and she is talking as usual."

Mom, Dad, Hunter, and Grandpa climbed down and joined Noah at the edge of the nest. From there they saw the little redheaded western girl, the small Sasquatch, and 7 large Sasquatch walking. The girl was repeatedly calling out, "they want you, they want you," as she walked with the group below and along the base of the valley cliff wall.

"I am taking Hunter and Noah down to the bottom and jumping into the water canal, like you three did last time to escape," said Mom. "No hairy beasts or little redheads will set a finger on them. Now, Noah and Hunter, I don't want any arguments about whether we are leaving. We are leaving now, got it? I have been through enough these last few days, and don't want to lose you, so come with me, now!"

"I am not too sure we should act so hastily," said Grandpa, "it might be better to let them go by and make our plans more mindfully."

As Grandpa finished talking, he saw the boys and their dad get up quickly and follow Mom down the tree. "Well, obviously we are listening to Mom and leaving," he muttered to himself, as he quickly caught up to the others.

Grandpa reached the edge of the irrigation canal, and reminded everyone to make sure their suits were fully sealed up in order to be watertight. "It might be a few hours before we reach the town, so we need to make sure we don't have any leaks like Noah experienced last time," he said. Grandpa then asked each person if they had checked their seals, and asked Noah twice, just to make sure. Once he was sure they were all good to go, Grandpa yelled out, "Jump!"

Everyone hit the water just as the little western girl and the Sasquatch came over the edge of the wall and saw them. As the girl saw them jump into the water, she shouted, "I didn't say it correctly, they don't just want you... they want to teach you!"

ABOUT THE AUTHOR

Patrick Talmadge Sr. has always been a late bloomer. His growth didn't cease until he was over 21 years old. He reached his pinnacle as a national and world-class masters middle-distance runner at the age of 37, when he won his first master's national track and field championship in the 800-meter run.

At 47, Patrick earned his Bachelor of Arts degree and made history as the oldest NCAA cross-country runner. Seven years later, at 54, he returned to college to pursue a Master's degree in Psychology. During this time, he ran the mile in track, once again setting a record as the oldest NCAA track and field runner. He received his Master's degree in Psychology at 57. At the age of 66, he embarked on his writing journey.

Patrick taught himself to read at the tender age of three and a half and has been an avid reader ever since. With a keen interest in all fields of science, science fiction, and fantasy, he amassed a wealth of knowledge that would later prove invaluable when he began writing. Throughout his 20s and 30s, Patrick devoured two to three books a day. Upon graduating from graduate school in 2011, he retired from competitive running and felt a growing desire to write the stories that had been simmering within him.

In November 2021, spurred on by the love of his life, Patrick began his writing career. By July 2023, he had completed an adult four-book science fiction series about Sasquatch, a four-book children's series on the same subject, and a standalone novel about a senior community that befriends a troupe of Sasquatch.

Patrick possesses a unique ability to write multiple stories simultaneously, allowing him to modify and adjust interconnected narratives for clarity when writing a series. With a bit of luck, Patrick will continue to pursue his passion for writing for the rest of his life, or at least until his computer gives out.

ALSO BY PATRICK TALMADGE

Hidden Mountain Chronicles

Sasquatch Race

Sasquatch Prison Diary

Tenino Caverns

Sasquatch Home Planet

Sasquatch Chronicles

Hunter and Noah vs. Sasquatch Vol. 1

Hunter and Noah vs. Sasquatch Vol. 2

Hunter and Noah vs. Sasquatch Vol. 3

Hunter and Noah vs. Sasquatch Vol. 4

Sasquatch Senior Community Series

Sasquatch Senior Community

Sasquatch Senior Community: Lois and Mel the Beginning

Sasquatch Senior Community: The Early Years

Sasquatch Senior Community: The Middle Years

AFTERWORD

Go to hangar1publishing.com to learn more about the Authors and stay up to date with their newest releases.

www.ingramcontent.com/pod-product-compliance
Lightning Source LLC
Chambersburg PA
CBHW061325120626
46546CB00007B/2672